The Next Level

Jess Settles on Maximizing Potential

foreword by Dan Gable

Text by Jess Settles

Foreword by Dan Gable

Design by InspirationArt & Scripture

Photographs by Jan Krieger and Lloyd Bender

Copyright © 1999 *The Next Level: Jess Settles on Maximizing Potential*
Copyright © 1999 by Jess Settles

All Rights Reserved

Design by
Melissa Furness
InspirationArt & Scripture

Photographs by
Lloyd Bender
Jan Krieger

Printing by
Nite Owl Printing
Printed in the United States of America

Binding by
Dilly Manufacturing

Acknowledgements to Carole Harder, Gary Close, Jim Goodrich, Bill Horn, Bub & Lugene Krieger, and J.T. Settles

No part of this book, including photographs, may be reproduced or copied without the express written consent of *The Next Level: Jess Settles on Maximizing Potential*.

First Edition

The Next Level: Jess Settles on Maximizing Potential may be purchased for educational, business, sales promotion, or fundraising events within your school or organization. To order additional copies of *The Next Level* or to schedule Jess Settles to speak at your church, school or business call **(319)257-3585** or fax **(319)257-6895**.

The Next Level came together because of the efforts of so many people. Special thanks go out to:

Dr. Tom Davis, Iowa's winningest Basketball Coach

George Wine, former Iowa Sports Information Director and author of *Hayden Fry A High Porch Picnic*

Chuck Offenburger, the original Iowa Boy and columnist for *The Iowan*

Dale Arnes, Manager of the Iowa Hawk Shop

Charles Edwards, CEO of InspirationArt & Scripture

Dave Christensen, former Elementary Principal and Mt. Pleasant Community School District Director of Instruction

Melissa Furness, Graphic Designer for InspirationArt & Scripture

---

Photographs

Jan Krieger is a rising star in freelance photography and co-owner of Two Women and a Camera. Jan and husband Bruce Kittle, an Iowa football captain on the 1982 Rose Bowl team, reside in Madison, Wisconsin, with their two children, Emma and George.

Lloyd Bender has been the official cameraman for the Iowa Hawkeyes the past 35 years. He covers numerous University of Iowa events, and his photographs are represented in media guides covering every sport. Lloyd lives in Iowa City, Iowa, with his wife, Becky, and children, Holiday, Christie, Melissa, and Laura.

F o r e w o r d

I feel it quite interesting that an athlete and coach in a sport that rivals the basketball season is writing this foreword. Actually, I am honored to do so. Reading the contents of *The Next Level* reminded me of how simple it is to understand becoming successful. Even though it is laid out quite briefly and concisely to its readers, it also makes me realize how difficult it is to actually apply its meaning. If it is so simple, why isn't everyone at the top of their game and profession? It is because *knowing* and actually *doing* are quite different. It took me a short period of time to read this book, but actually digesting it and applying its meaning in everyday life takes discipline, time commitments, and all else that most fall short of. Jess shows in this reading how one can go about and prepare for accomplishments and how he actually applied its understanding to help him succeed. He does so through a strong "faith" in his motives. Even though I know Jess had to struggle with several obstacles in his latter college years, I know with this approach he can best get to his "next level" of vision. But like I said earlier, the difficulty is in the application. Based on my experience with Jess and witnessing his time spent training in the wrestling room (biking, etc.) as well as on the basketball court, his chances are good. His already established good work ethic and attitude will make the difference. To make accomplishments, one must start with knowing the route, and this book exactly accomplishes that feat in a personalized manner.

Continued success, Jess!

Dan Gable

Ever since I started playing varsity basketball during my freshman year in high school, people have asked me for advice on what it takes to succeed. After I was named Big Ten Freshman of the Year in 1994, I received hundreds of letters from people wanting to know the secrets to my success and how I managed athletics with academics. It's an honor to be a role model and a privilege to have lived out a dream playing for the Hawkeyes.

I wrote *The Next Level* in the summer of 1994 in order to give you an inside glimpse of how commitment and hard work have paid off in my life and how the same principles I follow will work for you. It is now a short time away from the year 2000, and I've had a few setbacks in my career. It's taken a strong faith in God and some serious perseverance, but I wanted you to know my strategies before I was injured. My message has not changed just because some of my goals have been altered. The same principles still apply in my life today. I know you'll enjoy *The Next Level*, and I know it will help you in your effort for maximizing potential.

Thanks.

Jess Settles

C o n t e n t s

Introduction	1
Goals	5
Tunnel Vision	9
Overcoming Obstacles	13
Positioning	17
Weakness	21
Preparation	25
Give a Little to the Journey	31
Today	35
Destination	39

Introductio

The Next Level

      Every day growing up I pictured myself running up and down the floor wearing the Black and Gold, finishing a pass from B.J. Armstrong, throwing an alley-oop to Roy Marble, setting a pick for Bobby Hansen, or high fiving Ronnie Lester. Although it was a long shot, I believed that someday I could make my dream of playing for the Hawkeyes a reality.

      There is no question that the game of basketball has opened up more doors for me than I could have ever imagined. I've played basketball in Europe, Alaska, and Hawaii, and it all started with a simple dream. I've guarded NBA stars Michael Jordan, Grant Hill, and Juwan Howard and worked out with Mitch Richmond, Chris Mullin, Tim Hardaway, Chris Street, and Iowa All-American and Atlanta football star Tim Dwight. I've received advice from former Notre Dame football coach Lou Holtz, Chicago Bulls' coach Tim Floyd, ESPN's Dick Vitale, and Iowa's Legendary Three of Hayden Fry, Dr. Tom Davis, and Dan Gable. I've been introduced to

Jess Settles

Indiana's Bobby Knight, Heisman winner Paul Hornung, Iowa's best-ever quarterback Chuck Long, USA Olympic women's basketball coach Tera Vanderveer, Pittsburgh Steeler All-Pro running back Jerome Bettis, world champion gymnast Kim Zmeskal, award winning actress Julia Roberts, and NBA legends Larry Bird, Jerry West, and Magic Johnson.

I'd like to sit here and tell you that there is a magic formula for all of the success these people have had. The only formula I could come up with after spending time with them is that they have a burning desire to excel in everything they do. Not only are they concerned about winning the battle, they also want to win the battle within. They want to reach their maximum level of potential and set new standards. They are constantly searching for their own next level, studying their weaknesses, and trying to overcome them.

The Next Level has been written to try to tap into the **unlimited potential** every one of you has. It's about making it to the top and taking as many people with you as you can. It's about **dreams**, simple ones, that could change your life forever.

Jess Settles #4

Jess Settles

Goals

Goals are the foundation of the dreams and accomplishments we set out to conquer. They are the driving forces behind our successes. Short-term goals may require just a lap around the track, while long-term goals could take years of discipline and endurance to reach. No matter what race we're running in life, setting goals is the first step to finishing.

Many of us have been misinformed about the types of goals we should set and how we are supposed to reach them. We are unappreciative of our talents. The truth is that each one of us has been blessed with an enormous amount of individual skill. I know people who have tremendous musical, artistic, athletic, academic, communication, or business ability, but they don't set goals and go for them. One of the greatest tragedies in this world is people who waste their potential. Many kids today think the Big Time is out of reach. Maybe it is, but why not try to get there? Not many people would have guessed I would be playing Division I basketball,

The Next Level

coming from Winfield, Iowa, a town of one thousand. Dream big, and set your goals high.

Each day you roll out of bed, you've got to visualize where you're going. My goal has always been to play in the NBA. To reach that dream,

Jess   Settles

I've got to keep improving every day. Each morning I plan what I'm going to achieve for that day. Some days I work on my shot, and on other days, I might focus on ball handling. I'm not just going through the motions and hoping it all works out; I'm doing all I can to make it a reality. The future is not something that just happens; the future is something we make happen. To make it happen, we've got to break down our goals into chunks. I know that to be an NBA player, I must develop all of my skills. To do this, I set daily and weekly goals. I strive to be able to dribble two basketballs indefinitely with my eyes closed, and once I can do that, I strive to do it full speed. In that regard, I learn each new skill in steps, not all at once.

Goals should shape our lives. Reaching them is not guaranteed, but the struggle to reach them makes us better people. Playing for the Iowa Hawkeyes started as a simple goal. Playing in the NBA is my next goal. Goals are the first part of your personal race in whatever endeavor you choose, but they are only the beginning. The finish line is where you want to be.

Tunnel Vision

I firmly believe that in order to achieve the goals you set, you must be willing to give up many things along the way. As a skinny yet determined eighth grader, I made a commitment to myself to play Division I basketball. I knew in my heart that I could achieve that goal. I also knew that it would be one of the most demanding goals I could undertake. With only four years ahead of me to make my dream come true, I had no time to waste.

Tunnel vision is the key to reaching any goal. I discovered right away that the older I got, the more obstacles seemed to jump in and cloud my vision. With school and homework to deal with during the week and social commitments on the weekend, I found myself doing what others wanted me to do instead of practicing and improving my game. I knew I would have to give up some of today's pleasures if tomorrow's dreams were to become reality.

Jess Settles

I quit watching some of my favorite shows and started working out on Friday and Saturday nights instead of going out with friends. I rearranged my priorities and blocked out all the rest. When I got to college, the distractions intensified, but I never took my eyes off my goal to excel in basketball.

There is always something you can do with your time that doesn't pertain to your committed goal. For some people it might be sleeping in, going out with friends, watching too much TV, or just taking a day off. Although all of these things can be necessary, to avoid cheating yourself, you must visualize your future success and put in the time and work to get there. Every time I speak at a camp or work a clinic, I see numerous athletes who have the ability to play a role on a college team but have difficulty committing to their goals. When I go back to the same camp or clinic two years later, most of the players haven't improved, haven't sold out, and usually come up short.

You have to block out distractions that aren't assisting your efforts toward your goal. You're not going to reach every goal you set, but by putting time into your goals, you'll be fulfilled knowing you did all you could do.

Overcoming Obstacles

The Next Level

At one time or another, every successful person I know has had to overcome a serious obstacle while pursuing his or her dream. Michael Jordan was cut from his high school team. Walt Disney struggled to get people to invest in his Disneyland vision. The stigma I dealt with was coming from a small high school. No matter how I played at summer camps or how many recruiting letters I received, most people still doubted my ability to go from a class of 36 to competing in the Big Ten.

"Just wait until he plays against people his same size," people said. I didn't set out to prove anyone wrong, but I wasn't about to let doubt affect me. I knew in my mind that I could excel at the next level no matter whom I played against or who believed in me. I believed in myself.

The vision to succeed was always with me, and I approached each obstacle with the end goal in mind.

Jess Settles

Too many people give up because of a setback. We complain that we didn't have the opportunities or that we were somehow cheated. If Disney had given up after a few people criticized his dream, we wouldn't have the Magic Kingdom, one of my favorite places in the world. Overcoming obstacles and setbacks builds character. Because the odds were against me, my character strengthened, and I developed an intense drive to make it.

Your mind is your most powerful tool. Use it to dig down deep inside to convince yourself of your abilities. Don't always listen to your emotions, as they can be deceptive. Dealing with obstacles and trying to overcome them is never easy, but making it to the top becomes much more satisfying.

As an eighth grader, I was rarely challenged by anyone our team played. At 6'3", I was the "big fish in a little pond." I had seen many area athletes dominate their sports and win much praise, but when it came time to receive college scholarships, no colleges were really interested. I didn't want the same thing to happen to me. I noticed a trend with many athletes.

Positioning

They were satisfied with short-term success instead of taking risks and investing in their futures. They were content with dominating at a small school. I knew there were many players around the country better than I, and I wanted to find them.

The summer before my freshman year in high school, I attended Howard Garfinkel's Five Star Basketball Camp in Pittsburgh and went up against the nation's best. I watched a rising senior from Reston, Virginia, named Grant Hill dominate in front of many college coaches, among them North Carolina's Dean Smith and Duke's Mike Krzyzewski. I wasn't

concerned with failure, but more importantly, with how I stacked up. If I found I couldn't compete, I would've gone home and tried something else. Fortunately the week was a success, and my career took off from there.

Success won't find you; you must find it. The great players weren't going to come to me; I had to go to Five Star to find them. To put yourself in the right position, you're going to have to take risks. And risks usually force you out of your comfort zone. My first game at Five Star was in front of 100 college coaches. I was scared to death. But I loved the atmosphere, and by the end of the week I had developed a new comfort zone.

Will you settle with being a teacher with a bachelor's degree, or will you head back to school and get a master's? Will you be a good mechanic, or will you take a risk and become an entrepreneur, opening your own shop? For me, it was putting my game on the line at Five Star and risking failure. People will always criticize, and statistics will always lean against you, but someone's got to be the best, so why not you?

Taking risks and putting yourself in the right position pays great dividends. Sometimes it only takes one good camp or test to send you on your way. Coming up short is a part of life, but taking risks to make dreams come true is something you'll never regret.

Weakness

The Next Level

The most overrated word in our world is *talent*. Talent gets you recruited, but mastering your weaknesses gets you to the next level. In basketball, many high school All-Americans don't ever make it to the pros. The power dunk they counted on is shut down in college, and their short jumper doesn't exist. The explosive move with their strong hand gets cut off, and they don't have a consistent move with the weak hand.

The only way to keep improving is to build your weaknesses into strengths.

Jess Settles

That's why I like Coach Davis so much. He tells me my weaknesses and gives me a plan to overcome them. I'm not afraid to be told that I don't do something well. I want to know. Give me a summer, and I'll make it a strength. God-given talents make up the basic ingredients, but there is always someone out there who is blessed with more. Michael Jordan set the standard for all of basketball. Blessed with tremendous skill, he worked hard to master the fundamentals of the game. It's easy to think that Jordan was born the superstar he is, but I'd say he created a superstar.

The more success we achieve early in our careers, the more we tend to relax and take our eyes off our long-term goals. About the time we settle for the moment, someone across the hall passes us by. Usually weaknesses are the last thing we ever want to work on. We don't like staying up late studying our least favorite subject or working on our weak hand dribbling after practice. We like to go to the driving range and smash long drives instead of working alone with the sand wedge.

But when the game is on the line, we might find ourselves hitting from the bunker, and we'd better know how to get out. There comes a day in all our lives when we wish we would've spent more time working on the things we don't do well. The day *I stop* improving is the day I hang up the *sneaks*.

Jess Settles

Preparation is what has separated me from much of my competition. There have been weeks when I have taken 2000 shots in practice, only to take 10 shots in the game. That may seem wasteful to some people, but I'm not planning on missing any of the shots that count. When I step on the court, I want my mind and body ready. I want to know I've done everything I could to prepare for this moment. As a team member, I want my teammates, coaching staff, and family to know I'm ready to give my best effort. I want them to know they can count on me daily. Nowhere in my mind do I want to have any doubt, and good preparation helps eliminate those doubts.

Preparation

Jess Settles

The game is just like a test:

Preparation must be both physical and mental. I've always been one to study the great ones. I've read countless articles and watched hours of game tapes and videos on Michael Jordan and Larry Bird. From them I learned the values of staying in shape, working on my all-around game, and coming to play every night. Always prepared for any situation at any given moment, they are successful every night. By studying them in those early years, I learned the game, and those lessons have been critical to my improvement.

With so many great athletes to compete against in college, I can't just show up and expect to do well. I have to rely on more than my physical abilities. During my freshman year, I had the privilege of eating supper with B.J. Armstrong on a road trip to Northwestern. He taught me how to fine-tune my mental game by studying my opponents more carefully and even keeping notes on each one of them. I automatically became a better student of the game, and it paid huge dividends. My game became as much mental as physical, and it improved.

The Next Level

The more I study, the better I do.

My pre-game routine is always the same. Shoot-around is five hours before the game. The first thing I practice is ball handling with two basketballs. I keep my eyes closed throughout the entire routine so my muscle memory takes over. Coach calls us in for walk-throughs, and we go through our offensive and defensive sets. Throughout his explanations I'm alert, trying to pick up anything extra that can get my team a steal, a rebound, or some other kind of advantage. Many of our games come down to the wire, so each advantage we get can make the difference. We break off, finishing with ten minutes of shooting at each end of the court. I start in close with my shots, trying to find my rhythm. I gradually move back while shooting jumpers and finish my routine with three-pointers. After a couple of power moves and drives to the basket, I head to the free-throw line. By this time, most of the guys are on their way to pre-game meal. Not me. I am usually the last one to leave. With a manager rebounding, I often finish with a flurry of game-speed shots. I want to get a sweat up.

My pre-game meal consists of pasta and pancakes. I've eaten that since I was a kid. After eating, I have a little over an hour to spend at my apartment or hotel room. I lie down and read my Bible. I visualize the upcoming battle, but I stay relaxed. I realize I'm blessed to even be in this position, so it's a time to reflect.

I show up at the gym two hours before tip off. I want my muscles to be loose, so I take about forty minutes to stretch. It's also a time to concentrate on tonight's opponent. I stretch out, get taped, and put on my uniform. After one last look at the scouting report, I'm almost ready to go. The last thing I do is slip on my Nikes. When I give those shoestrings a yank, I become a player. The adrenaline is there, the intensity is there, and I can't wait to do battle.

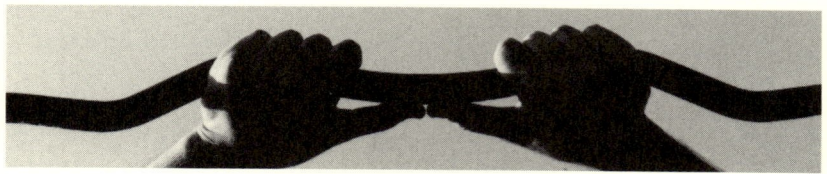

Preparation is a major factor for consistent success. Spend a moment with Iowa wrestling coach Dan Gable, and you'll see why he's the best ever. He's intense, he's prepared, and he's got you beat before you ever step on the mat.

There are always going to be some nights better than others, but being prepared will give you the *confidence* you need. No matter if it's a test, a presentation, or an athletic event, consistent *success* is going to come from preparation. Get a **dream**, get a routine, and get after it.

The Next Level

I've never known anyone who has accomplished his or her dream without a lot of help along the way. No individual or team ever gains success with just one person. It takes people sacrificing for each other to complete the task at hand. When you've been given a gift, share it with other people. Help other people grow with you.

In our highly competitive world, we often want to stand on the podium alone, but there is plenty of room for everyone.

Jess   Settles

Whether it's playing catch with a child, helping your little sister tie her shoes, thanking someone, or complimenting a teammate, everyone has an opportunity to give a little on their journey through life. In basketball, there have been many superstars unable to figure out that this is a team game. The great ones realize that making the extra pass and encouraging their teammates brings huge benefits. The team wins and everyone shines. It is the same in life. Everyone loves to be around a genuine person who doesn't always have his or her own agenda in mind.

We all know someone we could *encourage* at this moment with a phone call, a letter, a game of golf, or a simple wink. There are so many *opportunities*.

So *give* a little to the journey, and make the day of someone who needs you.

Today is your day. Every week in the world of sports, a major upset takes place. Whether it's lack of preparation, a hostile environment, or just a bad day at the office, upsets are bound to happen. With the fans and media always looking ahead to the marquee match-ups, it's hard for teams and individuals not to overlook the team they should easily dominate on paper. It's something a coach warns against constantly.

As individuals, we also tend to get too far ahead of ourselves. We're always living for the weekend or the next paycheck, and like teams that don't take care of business today, we end up falling short of our long-term goals.

The only guarantee we have is today; tomorrow will come if we're fortunate.

T o d a y

Iowa assistant basketball Coach Rich Walker had a powerful conversation with me that helped me put my goals in perspective. He told me that every morning he wakes up with a plan to succeed *today*. He wants to go to bed knowing he did all he could do with the day he had.

> That is what makes good players great and great players legends. They play every day like it is their last chance. They do drills as if time is running out on them. They are...

encouragers, believers, and they **make things happen.** They aren't worried about yesterday; it's gone. They don't get stressed about tomorrow because it may never come. If there's a long-term goal you're striving for, start by succeeding **today.**

Destination

The Next Level

I decided at an early age that I wanted to be a Big Ten athlete. When my father met with Miss Asby, my fifth grade teacher, years ago at a parent-teacher conference, she told him I was destined to be an Iowa Hawkeye, and she really thought I'd make it. I guess she knew I had the drive and had already started my quest. At that point in my life, I was more worried about the kickball game at recess than playing Indiana, but the motivation to excel was there.

I don't believe automatic success is anyone's destiny, but I believe with hard work you are destined to succeed.

I had faith that God would take me where He wanted me to go, and I was going to work my tail off for Him. It takes hours of practice to reach your full potential. I've heard that "overnight success" takes about 15 years. No one except you and God knows if you're giving everything you've got.

You may never have 15,500 people cheering for you in Carver Hawkeye Arena, but that isn't what's important. Enjoyment in life comes from reaching your own next level and helping others reach theirs. I've been living my dream for the last decade. Someday you'll be living yours. Work hard and believe, and your destination is right down the road.

Goals

Strengths

Weaknesses to Improve

Obstacles to Overcome

*I can do all things through
him who strengthens me.*
Phillipians 4:13